PROCESS THEOLOGY AND MYSTICISM

BRUCE EPPERLY

Energion Publications
Gonzalez, Florida
2023

ISBN: 978-1-63199-885-0
eISBN: 978-1-63199-886-7

Energion Publications
1241 Conference Rd
Cantonment, FL 32533

energion.com
pubs@energion.com

This text is dedicated to my teacher

David Ray Griffin (1939-2022),

whose theological adventures
inspired my own adventurous theological spirit.

TABLE OF CONTENTS

CHAPTER ONE

MYSTIC PROCESS

The power by which God sustains the world is the power of himself as the ideal…the world lives by its incarnation of God in itself.[1]

Process theology is mystical theology. In the world described by process-relational theology, the heavens declare the glory of God and so does every cell in our bodies (Psalm 19:1). As the Energy of Love and the Aim Toward Beauty, God moves in all things, including the depths of the unconscious mind and the heights of self-transcendent spirit. For philosopher Alfred North Whitehead, the parent of process-relational theology, "the teleology of the universe is aimed at the production of beauty."[2] We experience this drive toward beauty whether we are gazing through the lens of a microscope or at photographs from the Hubble and Webb telescopes. God is in all things and, more remarkably, all things are in God. The word lives by the incarnation of God and finds healing in God's creative-responsive love which inspires our partnership with God in healing the world.

Dramatic encounters with God give birth to and continue to sustain the world's religions and transform our lives. God is equally present in the "ordinary": our beating hearts, immune system, and five senses. The secular is sacred, and the sacred permeates the secular. We can experience God in the more dramatic moments of a voice speaking from a burning bush, angelic encounter, revelatory dream, or moment of inspiration. We can also encounter the Holy in taking our blood pressure, filling our plastic pill case, comforting a frightened child, cooking breakfast for a companion, or pondering the meaning of a dream. Dramatic or quotidian, God is incarnate in our lives, making everything miraculous, as poet Walt Whitman declares.

---

1 Alfred North Whitehead, *Religion in the Making* (New York: Meridian Books, 2000), 149.
2 Alfred North Whitehead, *Adventures in Ideas* (New York: Free Press, 1967), 265.

Process theologians affirm the wisdom of Celtic spiritual guides who believed that all places are potentially "thin places," transparent to divinity and manifesting the miraculous for those who open their doors of perception and then see everything as it is — as infinite. Grounded in divine adventure, all things find their home in God, as they are received into the ever-expanding and dynamic "consequent nature" of God, the all-embracing and ever-expanding memory of "the one to whom all hearts are open, and all desires known."

The complex and challenging philosophical and theological terminology of process theology points to the basic reality that life itself is a miracle, and that all things, even moments of pain and conflict, bear the imprint of divinity and can become the media of spiritual transformation. The natural world of cause and effect is more amazing and energetic, and also more creative, than we can ever imagine. God comes to us in all things. All things, even the painful and inconvenient, reveal something, albeit opaquely, of God's vision of healing and wholeness.

Mystic Moments. Process theology affirms that mysticism is concrete and personal. The Infinite is Intimate. The Cosmic is Companionable. In a time of national crisis, Isaiah enters the Jerusalem Temple and encounters the God of the Universe sitting on the throne. Angelic beings sing, "Holy, holy, holy is the Lord of hosts; the whole earth is full of his glory." God queries the astonished prophet-in-waiting, "Whom shall I send, and who will go for us?" The amazed Isaiah responds, "Here am I; send me!" (Isaiah 6:1-8). Mysticism begets prophetic ministry. The God of the Universe is concerned with the price of food, farm foreclosures, hospitality to immigrants, racism, and the exploitation of women.

Doing chores at home, young Mary receives an angelic visitor, who gives her an amazing task, birthing God's Child, and she responds with "yes." Mary Magdalene, grief-stricken at her spiritual friend's death comes to the Garden alone, hears the voice of the resurrected Jesus call her name, and is inspired to become an apostle herself. And, to your surprise, today, you may pause to notice the world around you while coffee is brewing and for a moment realize:

This is my *Parent's* world.
And to my listening ears
All nature sings, and round me rings
The music of the spheres.[3]

Suddenly transfigured and lifted to a higher spiritual plane, you go back to the kitchen, pour yourself a cup of coffee, fix your children their school lunches, hurry to get them to the bus stop on time, and negotiate traffic on the way to work, knowing that you are part of the Universe Story, a child of the universe, at home in the world to which you are called to bring beauty and love to each encounter. You go about "ordinary life," forever changed. None of your work companions or parents at the bus stop may notice it but from now on the quotidian events of life will be chockful of divinity. Children's messes and carpools to sports and school open the door to the wardrobe leading to Narnia and the path that leads to Gate 9 ¾ and Hogwarts' world of wizardry and magic. In that brief moment of domestic mystical illumination, you feel the subtle call to become a love finder, light bearer, and justice seeker in the ordinary moments of daily life and your responsibility as a global citizen. You now wear the mantle of the two Mary's and mystics throughout history. With Franciscans through the centuries, your constant plea at the supermarket, workplace, or while listening to the news now becomes "God, make me an instrument of your peace."

A Virtue in Vagueness. "There is a virtue in vagueness," counseled Rev. John Deason, Interim Minister at First Presbyterian Church in Mount Pleasant Michigan. In the summer of 1980, as I began my first full-time teaching position at Central Michigan University, the congregation split over issues related to the authority of scripture and the role of women as congregational leaders. That Sunday, the preacher was reminding those who remained that claiming to have absolute certainty about our understanding of scripture and doctrine leads to schism and the demonizing of our opponents. We should seek the truth and must always remember that our understanding of truth is always finite, fallible, and

---

3 "This is My Father's World," Maltbie Babcock. (author's paraphrase)

subject to change. This is good news for theologians and spiritual seekers. We are all mystics, and in the spirit of the image of the blindfolded or sight-impaired persons grasping different aspects of the elephant, we only comprehend a portion of the Holy even in our most illumined and life transforming experiences.

The spiritual life is a constant process of growing in wisdom and stature, and inclusion and awareness. As philosopher William James rightly observes, there are a variety religious experiences. God is always more than we can fathom or imagine. We can describe our encounters with God, and also affirm their ineffability, or indescribability, as well as the limitations of our experiences of the Holy. Moreover, to our chagrin, our sense of the Holy comes and goes, often choked by the weeds of busyness and anxiety.

One of my spiritual mentors Howard Thurman described mysticism as the immediate awareness of the Holy. "Mysticism is defined as the response of the individual to a personal encounter with God within his own soul" that shapes "the inner quality of the life and its outward expression as its manifestation."[4] Alfred North Whitehead, the philosophical parent of process theology, spoke of religion as what an individual does with their solitariness, and yet the philosopher equally affirmed that the whole universe conspires to create each moment of experience, including moments of mystical illumination.[5]

Authentic spirituality begins and ends with experiencing the Holy. Although encounters with the Holy necessitate philosophical and theological reflection, our reflections must be grounded in experience and always take us back to the experiences that gave birth to our spiritual traditions. God touches all of us. Each moment emerges from God's vision and energy and aims at the beauty and wholeness with which God inspires creation. Each moment arises from the ambient as well as immediate environment, the unconscious as well as the transpersonal, which reflects in greater or lesser degrees the impact of Holy. There are, as Sufi mystic

---

4   Howard Thurman, *Mysticism and Social Action* (London, International Association for Religious Freedom, 2014), Kindle, 174.

5   Alfred North Whitehead, *Religion in the Making* (New York: Meridian Press, 1960), 4.

Rumi counsels, a hundred ways to kneel and kiss the ground, and a myriad ways to experience the Holy.

Process theology asserts that God addresses us personally and individually, and also concretely, in relationships and history. We arise in our own unique time and place, experiencing God's mercies freshly with each new morning (Lamentations 3:22-23). Mystical experiences involve alignment with God's personal vision for our lives and a sense of intimacy with a Personal God. Mystical experiences also emerge non-theistically from our wonder at the universe, and sense of radical amazement and gratitude for the wonder of all being, and the holy ground upon which we walk. "Bidden or unbidden God is present," Swiss psychiatrist Carl Jung posts on the door of his Zurich home, quoting Erasmus. God is here and when the doors of perception are cleansed, we realize that we always stand on Holy Ground.

Definitional vagueness reflects the abundant and varied presence of the Holy, addressing us in many ways and through many avenues of experience. From the process perspective, mysticism involves the conscious awakening to the divinity and holiness of Life, the wonder of all Being and Becoming, flowing in and through us to all creation, guiding our steps and opening us to the universe. Although mystics may seek times of solitary contemplation and appear to the outsider to abandon the ebb and flow of domestic life, ultimately process-relational mysticism deepens our empathy and sense of connection with life's challenges. Mysticism inspires self-transcendence in which our isolated egos find peace, perspective, and power in connection and loyalty to the world beyond ourselves.

From the perspective of process theology, there are burning bushes to be found on every highway. Light glimmers through fall foliage and inspiration guides our steps when we least anticipate it. According to process theology the omnipresent and omni-active God is initially present in the primordial unconscious origins of each moment of experience. Through God's initiative and our intentional openness, we bring the Holy to consciousness.

Mystical moments are always concrete and personal, and embodied and intimate. While our encounters with the Divine have common elements, they are also intensely pluralistic in nature as we grasp different aspects of the living, changing divine elephant. Some mystics experience dazzling darkness, others are transformed by God's grandeur. Still, other mystics, like Isaiah and Amos, receive the call to prophetic protest.

God and the ambient universe from which our lives emerge are diverse and plural in their manifestations. Accordingly, mystical experiences must be equally plural and diverse, grounded in our varied cultures, religious traditions, and personalities as well as the many aspects of God or the Ultimate reality "in whom we live and move and have our being" (Acts 17:28). Mystical experiences also vary according to the seasons of life from childhood to senior adulthood. We receive the illumination and guidance we need to experience the Divine possibility that is most inspiring and appropriate to our age, personality and life situation.

Exploring The Mystic Path. The mystic's journey emerges from the interplay of divine call and human response and reflects our unique and intimate experiences of the Holy. In her classic on mysticism, Evelyn Underhill describes the mystic journey as involving the interplay of awakening, purgation, illumination, the dark night, and union.[6] The mystic path involves both expansion of consciousness and simplification of focus. Creation theologian Matthew Fox speaks of four ways of mystical adventure: the way of wonder (*via positiva*), the way of suffering and simplicity (*via negativa*), the way of creativity and agency (*via creativa*), and the way of transformation *(via transformativa)*. Fox sees the mystic path as profoundly relational and transformational in its integration of personal growth and social responsibility. The transpersonal nature of mystical experiences finds its fulfillment in facing the particular challenges of daily life, political involvement, and care for the planet.[7] While Underhill represents a more traditional description of the mystic's path, the British mystic, influenced by Whitehead's philosophy, recognizes that mysticism is profoundly practical in expression. Our awakening to God leads to drawing away from the temptations of the world to better experience God's

6 Evelyn Underhill, *Mysticism* (New York: Image Press, 1990).
7 Matthew Fox, *Original Blessing* (Los Angeles: TarcherParagree, 2000).

presence in the complexities of our lives as the prelude to union with God and all things.

My process-relational approach to the mystic path joins the wisdom of both Underhill and Fox. Mystics can be both contemplatives and activists, joining prayer and meditation with a commitment social transformation and prophetic protest. Awakened by divine illumination they discover that wherever God is hidden, God needs to be unearthed and revealed in our responses to the tragic beauty of daily life and citizenship, and this often means tearing down the walls of injustice to let God's light shine through.

The mystical path of process theology can be described in terms of the dynamic interplay of awakening, affirming, simplifying, expanding, and transforming.

Awakening to God's grandeur illuminating all creation. Mystics discover God's light shining in every person and all creation. In the spirit of Jacob's dream at Beth-El, "the house of God," they discover, "God was in this place — that is, every place — and now I know it" (Genesis 28:17, AP).

» *Affirming the Universe as a Reflection of Divinity in Body, Mind, and Spirit.* This world in all its tragic beauty and perpetual perishing matters and is, as John Calvin avers, the theatre of divine glory. Process mysticism leads to world-affirmation. God loves our cells as well as our souls. God nurtures our spiritual hungers and wants us to feed the hungry. The pathway to mystical awareness begins in the complexities of daily life and citizenship. Divine omnipresence challenges us to embrace the joys and sorrows of the world as an inspiration to release the holiness, imprisoned and disguised by unjust social structures.

» *Simplifying Our Focus and Decluttering Our Spirit.* Traditionally identified with the path of purgation, the mystic's commitment to simplicity of life prunes away the clutter that stands between us and God. Jesus proclaimed that he is the vine, and we are the branches. God trims all the dead branches so that God's spiritual energy will flow unobstructed in and through us to the world (John 15:1-8). The quest for simplicity opens us to experiencing God's moment by moment and long-term vision, "the initial aim," in our lives and in the world around us. Simplicity of life joins us with God and God's children, most especially those who lack life's basics. By practicing simplicity, we become good stewards of our economies and ecologies.

» *Expanding Our Compassion and Empathy.* Spiritual growth involves expanding our spirits so that our well-being and the well-being of others become joined. Process mysticism inspires empathy and connection, not apathy and isolation. Loving our neighbor as ourselves, we see our neighbor's joy as contributory to our own fulfillment and enhanced by our compassionate care. Spiritual stature involves jettisoning the solitary ego and the prison of rugged individualism to embrace world loyalty. Large spirited, we claim our vocation as little Christs and Bodhisattvas, God's companions in healing the world.

» *Transforming Ourselves and Our World.* God calls us to become new creations, not conformed to this world, but transformed by the renewing of our minds. (Romans 12:2) Each moment is a healing moment joining personal and global healing. While mystics seek personal equanimity amid the storms of life, they also feel a divine restlessness, grounded in their experience of the distance between our world and God's aim at Shalom. Mystics are way makers and world shapers, regardless of the scope of their responsibilities. We commit ourselves to what the Eastern Church describes as *theosis,* or divinization, becoming God-awakened through letting God's vision inspire our vision.

Inspired by divine dynamism, mystics never stand still. Their mystical adventures mirror God's providential and provocative movements through history, challenging injustice and luring us toward God's peaceable realm.

LIVING PROCESS MYSTICISM.

I am a prophet of process theospirituality: the affirmation that spirituality and theology emerge in dynamic interdependence.

8

Deep down and whether we are currently aware of it, we are all touched by God and are all mystics, capable of transpersonal or illuminative experiences. The panentheistic affirmation, "God in all things," inspires us to seek God in every experience and encounter. Accordingly, each chapter will conclude with a spiritual practice aimed at nurturing mystical experiences in the spirit of process theology. The corresponding panentheistic affirmation, "All things in God," motivates us to do something beautiful for God and the world around us, and making our lives our gift to God.

To ground your sense of God's presence, throughout the day, pause, take a few breaths, and then notice the holiness of yourself and life around you. Let your senses bathe themselves in beauty. "Taste and see" that God is good (Psalm 34:8). Inhale the aromas of holiness. Caress the "God with skin," your skin, the skin of a beloved companion, the feel of water or fabric. Listen to God speaking through the morning praise of birds, rain beating against a window, and crashing waves. Take a moment to see the divine light peeking through your companions, friends, family, and strangers you encounter. Let your day be guided by the intention to see the light and then bring forth the divine light in yourself, others, and every situation.

Process mysticism gives birth to a "woke" spirituality in which drawing near to God increases our sense of relationship with others. While solitariness is essential to spiritual growth, our solitude is relational and opens us to the greater empathy. For example, each morning after turning on my coffee maker and going outside to greet the morning (in my case around 4:30 a.m.), I center myself through contemplative prayer. I conclude my centering meditation with a brief spoken prayer, "God, awaken me to beauty and help me to add to the joy and beauty of the world today." I visualize my family and persons dealing with challenges and then look at my online newsfeed with a prayerful spirit. Most mornings, I take a three-to-four-mile predawn prayer walk. I begin my walk with the words of the Psalmist, "this is the day that God has made, and I will rejoice and be glad in it" (Psalm 118:24) and the first line of the Prayer of St. Francis, "God, make me an instrument of your peace," and commit myself to be a peacemaker and light bearer in my family life, daily activities, and political involvement. When I call a political representative to urge them to support a justice or climate related cause, I say a silent prayer to join my prophetic advocacy with a healing spirit.

CHAPTER TWO

ADVENTURES IN THEOSPIRITUALITY

God confronts the actual with what is possible for it ...
Every act leaves the world with a deeper or fainter impress of
God. God then passes in his next relationship to the world with
enlarged, or diminished, presentation of ideal values.[8]

Whitehead was a master in creating innovative language or using familiar words in novel ways to describe his vision of the universe. Apart from Whitehead's *Process Reality* and texts penned by process theologians or philosophers, we seldom hear words such as "prehension," "concrescence," "hybrid physical feelings," "subjective aim," "primordial, consequent, and superjective nature of God," to name but a few of Whitehead's neologisms, virtually incomprehensible to laypersons.[9] Accordingly, I have kept technological language to a minimum in this text and have focused on living process theology, converting the linguistic creativity of Whiteheadian language to everyday conversation and spiritual experience.

Whitehead believed he needed to stretch language to the limits to portray the wondrous complexity of cosmological thinking. Unlike many of his philosophical peers, Whitehead believed that the quest for wisdom — and understanding our universe — must take into consideration the totality of experience. Thoughts and emotions, scientific investigations, unconscious feelings, moral and spiritual inclinations, and mystical and paranormal experiences must undergird our philosophical reflections. Whitehead recognized that the great religions, and the mystical experiences upon which they are grounded, seek to illuminate the totality of experience as well as provide guidance for our personal, institutional, and moral decision-making. We must go to the mountain-

---

8 Alfred North Whitehead, *Religion in the Making*, 153, 152. (inclusive language)

9 One of my theological mentors has written a guide to the Whiteheadian nomenclature. John B. Cobb, *Whitehead Word Book: A Glossary with Alphabetical Index to Technical Terms in Process and Reality* (Claremont: Process Century Press, 2015).

top to see God's movements in the moral and spiritual arcs of history. We must also look for God's messy incarnation in conflicts at work and in the push and pull of advocacy for justice and earth care.[10] The Cosmos and the Congress equally reveal the presence of God for those who attend to God's aims at truth, beauty, and goodness. Attentive to the Poet of the Universe, even politics can become poetic.

Process theologian David Ray Griffin believed that deep down everyone seeks to be in harmony with the universe. The universe is not aimless or value neutral but is aimed at the production of beauty, grounded in the emergence of complexity and intensity of experience, whether this involves the evolution of galaxies, planets, and societies or the intricacies of our daily peregrinations. The moral and spiritual arcs of the universe flow through persons as well as institutions. There is something of the divine, to use the language of Quakers, in every moment of experience.

God is the ultimate source of the order of the universe upon which we depend for our existence. God is also the source of the ideals that energize the quest for knowledge, wisdom, science, holiness, and justice. Present both beyond and within the universe, God can be described as the Poet of the Universe, guiding the world with the divine vision of truth, goodness, and beauty and inviting us to play our part as poetic and prophetic companions in healing the earth one moment at a time.

Deep down, all creatures experience the impact of God in their process of self-creation. This is the basis of religious experience and moral reflection. Indeed, as mystics believe, it is possible to experience God directly in moments of spiritual enlightenment and empathy. We also experience God in terms of apprehending the orderly processes of the universe, intuiting the divine purposes for particular moments of experience, and feeling the divine pathos, God's emotional response to the sorrow and joy, injustice and healing, of persons and institutions.[11]

I employ the innovative term "theospirituality" to describe the heart of process theology and its metaphysical vision. Process

10 Bruce Epperly, *Messy Incarnation: Meditations on Christ in Process* (Gonzalez, FL: Energion, 2022).
11 Abraham Joshua Heschel, *The Prophets* (New York: Harper, 2001).

theology articulates a vision of the universe, grounded in and responsive to transcendent and transpersonal experiences, that is, experiences of the Holy. Lively and dynamic in perspective, process theology constantly opens us to new visions of reality and novel ways to experience God. While theological concepts are important, they are always finite, fallible, and subject to transformation. Tragically, theologians and spiritual leaders often freeze and isolate what is intended to be dynamic and relational, leading to fixation on past experiences and outmoded world views and the silencing of minority voices. Theological affirmations must always be grounded in the concreteness of lived experience and tested by their ability to illuminate the moral and spiritual arcs of personal and planetary history.

With full awareness of the dynamic nature of life and the fallibility and limitation of every theological perspective, I believe the heart of process theospirituality and mysticism, can be described by the following experience-based affirmations:

» *We live in a dynamic, ever-changing universe, grounded in the loving creativity of a faithful and ever-changing God.* God's vision of truth, beauty, and goodness is embodied in dynamic processes of creative transformation. Immanent within the world, God can be experienced as our deepest reality and as the goal inspiring our spiritual journey. It is impossible *not* to experience the divine. Even our turning away from God reflects, albeit in a confused way, divine providential love. Mystics experience God's presence as definitive of the dynamic flow of personal, communal, and planetary history and as constitutive of their identity.

» *Reality is interdependent and interactive, reflecting the divine call and creaturely response.* While religion is, as Whitehead says, "what an individual dues with *their* solitariness," the solitude of spiritual contemplation emerges from the movements of God that give birth to each moment of experience.[12] The whole universe, including God, provides the foundation for each moment of experience. As the energy of love that holds the universe together, God enables us to experience ho-

12 Alfred North Whitehead, *Religion in the Making*, 6.

liness in unity and diversity, and to embrace the gentle, and sometimes tempestuous, relatedness of life. An intricate relational universe is characterized by non-local as well as local causation. We can experience what is near at hand, revealed in memory, the influence of our bodies, and the actions of our companions. We can also intuit experiences at a distance, the emotions and thoughts of others, and be affected by the prayers of others. Our own prayers and good intentions are non-local in nature. They shape to a greater or lesser degree the wellbeing of those for whom we pray, regardless of distance. The intricate interdependence of life, described by the terms "quantum entanglement" and the "collective unconscious" make paranormal experiences of joining with others and telepathic communication as well as answers to prayer plausible.

» *We live in an enchanted universe in which everything that breathes can praise God and God is present as the loving energy in all things.* There are, as Celtic spiritual guides asserted, thin places everywhere. Divine energy and wisdom permeate our cells and our souls. Every creature is a word of God, a theophany, reflecting divine creativity. Every creature and encounter can be a source of revelation and inspiration. The universe — and our humble planet — is full of God's glory. For those whose senses are open and whose hearts and minds are awakened, God greets us in the face of each creature. Mystical experience is normal rather than an aberration or supernatural.

» *Divine creativity is mirrored in the creativity of God's creation, both human and non-human.* The universe is, at every level, a theatre for creative transformation. To be is to create. We are artists of experience whose artistry mirrors the creativity of the poet of the universe. Spiritual transformation inspires creativity and transformation in our lives and the world around us.

» *We live in a meaningful and beautiful universe.* Isaiah encounters God in the temple and discovers that "whole earth is full of God's glory" (Isaiah 6:3). The aim of the universe is at the production of beauty.[13] Everything that exists reflects divine wisdom. Despite the impact of accident and mistake, we are at home in the universe. This truly is our Parent's world, as the hymn proclaims:

This is my *Parent's* world:
I rest me in the thought
Of rocks and trees, of skies and seas—
God's hand the wonders wrought.[14]

» *God is our closest companion.* Alfred North Whitehead describes God as the "fellow sufferer who understands" and the loving companion who celebrates.[15] God is in all things and all things are in God. God is within us as the inspiration to seek beauty and justice. Our lives are our gifts to God who treasures each moment of experience, allowing Godself to be shaped by our lives. This is the divine pathos reflected in God's empathetic awareness of humanity, social structures, and the non-human world. From our finite and fallible perspective, we can humbly bring to consciousness the intentions and emotions of divinity and ascertain God's vision for our lives and the world around us.

» *As the Poet of the Universe, God is the source of novelty and change. Following God inspires a spirituality that treasures the past, including our traditions and rituals. God's Spirit, joining gentleness and restlessness beckons us, to new horizons of faithfulness.* Ever faithful and constant in love, God is constantly doing a new thing. God's mercies are new every morning. Not locked in the past, God calls us toward new possibilities. When we respond to God's call, we shape God's next response to the world. God is the ultimate relativist and change agent, addressing and responding to each creature personally and intimately. God leads the world forward with visions emerging

---

13 Alfred North Whitehead, *Adventures in Ideas,* 265.
14 "This is My Father's World," Maltie Babcock.
15 Alfred North Whitehead: *Process and Reality* (New York: Free Press, 1979).

in dialogue with our present personal, congregational, family, national, and planetary situation as well as God's long-term vision for us and our communities. Mysticism treasures the past and delights in the changing shapes of divine creativity manifest in our lives and every creature. The moral and spiritual arcs of the universe call us forward to new horizons of justice-seeking and peacemaking.

» *God is the Artist of the Universe, leading us forward in the quest to embody divine truth, goodness, healing, and beauty in the world.* The mystic is a spiritual artist reflecting the delight that the Divine Artist takes in our creativity. Think of the poetry of Julian of Norwich and Rumi, the dance of the Sufis and First Americans, the music of Hildegard of Bingen, the courage of St. Patrick, and the visionary writing of William Blake and the Bhagavad Gita. Our creativity reflects our fidelity to the divine poetry. God wants us to create and to do new things. Like an empathetic and supportive parent, God says, "surprise me, bring something new into the world, something I hadn't fully imagined!" When we create, we add to God's impact in the world. Our artistry whether in music, language, the visual arts, politics, theological reflection, spiritual experience, or service reflects our vocation as intimate companions in God's aim at beauty. In synch with God's vision, we take our place as God's creative companions in healing and beautifying the world.

Process theology and theospirituality is always in process and incomplete. In words Thomas of Celano employed to describe Francis of Assisi, process mysticism is "always new, always fresh, always beginning again." The flow of the Spirit inspires us to explore new forms of theological reflection and spiritual practice. The mystic heart of process theospirituality is always beating, energizing, and imagining new possibilities as we encounter new aspects of God's relationship with the world. The horizons of spirituality and theology are always expanding, most especially as we grow spiritually, compassionately, and intellectually. God is more than we can imagine. The universe contains mysteries and marvels beyond calculation. The wonder of life coursing within us is infinite in its loving intimacy.

LIVING PROCESS MYSTICISM

We live in a God-filled universe, in which everything that breathes, praises God (Psalm 148, Psalm 150:6). "Even the stars pray," as process theologian Jay McDaniel avers. We are all mystics, but simply don't *yet* know it!

Mystical experiences come dramatically and unexpectedly to persons like Moses, Isaiah, Saul of Tarsus, and Mary of Magdala. To others, mystic breakthroughs come as a result of a commitment to spiritual practices such as meditation, prayer, chanting, and dream work. Life is a dynamic relationship in which God constantly and intimately calls and, to varying degrees, we respond.

You can embrace "the mystic in you" through what I describe as a "light meditation." Find a comfortable spot and begin gently breathing, feeling the universe entering you with each breath. Connected with all things, begin to visualize a divine light entering you with each breath, the light of creation, the energy of love, your deepest identity. Feel the light filling your whole being, from the top of your head to your toes. Experience the light enlivening your body and enlightening with your spirit. Experience yourself as "the light of the world" (Matthew 5:13-16). Now, as you exhale, experience the divine light within you flowing out into the world, bringing peace and healing, as you "let your light shine."

Throughout the day, pause to breath in God's light. Claim your vocation as a "light giver," enlightened by God and called to bring enlightenment and healing to every situation. Pause to see the light in others and guided by Divine Light, bring forth the light in others.

CHAPTER THREE

GOD AND THE MANY FACES OF MYSTICISM

> *By SIZE I mean the stature of a person's soul, the range*
> *and depth of his love, his capacity for relationships. I mean the*
> *volume of life you can take into your being and still maintain*
> *your integrity and individuality, the intensity and variety of*
> *outlook you can entertain in the unity of your being without*
> *feeling defensive or insecure. I mean the strength of your spirit*
> *to encourage others to become freer in the development of their*
> *diversity and uniqueness.*[16]

Since college in the early 1970's, I have been inspired by the story of the sight impaired or blindfolded persons and their quest to understand the nature of an elephant. According to the legend, each of the sight impaired persons experiences a part of the elephant, and claims that their experience fully describes this mighty and mysterious creature. In succession, each compares the creature to a rope, a tree trunk, a sword, and a wall, depending on the part they are touching. Yet, the elephant is far more than any one part.[17]

The original story, emerging in South Asia, points to the elephant as the ultimate reality and serves as an invitation to explore the many aspects of the Ultimate Reality. Spiritual seekers are reminded that perspective is everything: our cultural, spiritual, historical, and social location shapes how we experience the Holy. Rather than daunting the spiritual seeker, the image of God as dynamic and beyond any particular spiritual tradition inspires us to a lifetime of growing, as Jesus did, in wisdom and stature. Like the story of the mysterious and multi-faceted elephant, the Sufi poet Rumi counsels us to delight in the liberating journey to God,

---

16 Bernard Loomer, "S-I-Z-E is the Measure," Henry James Cargas and Bernard Lee, *Religious Experiences and Process Theology* (Mahweh, NJ: Paulist Press, 1976), 70.

17 I discuss the nature of religious pluralism in Epperly, *The Elephant is Running: Process and Open and Relational Theology and Religious Pluralism* (New York: SacraSage, 2022).

whose many faces take us from books and doctrines to praise and enlightenment:

> Today, like every other day, we wake up frightened.
> Don't open the door to the study and begin reading. Take
> down a musical instrument. Let the beauty we love, be
> what we do. There are a hundred ways to kneel and kiss the
> ground.

Awakening to the wondrous diversity of the Dynamic Divinity opens the portals of our hearts, minds, and spirits, to beauty, love, empathy, and healing beyond what we can ask or imagine. It sets us on a never-ending journey into Divinity.

Yet, there is another aspect to the story of the sight-impaired persons and the elephant. A living elephant is constantly on the move, walking, communicating, flapping its tail and ears. A living God is also on the move, revealing different aspects of the Divine moment by moment. The eternal and timeless nature of God — God's primordial nature — is constantly being adjusted in relationship to a changing world and in concert with God's own intentionality.[18]

While the mystic quest takes us far beyond institutional Christianity or any other spiritual tradition, the Christian vision of Trinity points to the wondrous diversity of God whose creative and responsive love addresses each of us personally, encountering us uniquely with the divine aspect that meets our unique need, social and religious location, and spiritual maturity. The many faces of God awaken us to a multitude of spiritual paths. The Hindus speak of these paths as yogas, personally and religiously suited to age, temperament, and social location. There are yogas oriented toward physical wellbeing, contemplation, intellectual acuity, political involvement, energy, and praise and worship. There is a path for every person, and every person can experience union with the Ultimate on the path to which they are called. As we journey toward God, new horizons of Divinity open up as God walks beside us. We can rejoice in the faith of Christian mystic and author

---

18 Whitehead also describes the ongoing consequent and superjective natures of God, God's embrace of all things and sharing of God's experience with the world in terms of divine possibility and experience.

Madeleine L'Engle, who confessed, "I do not think I will ever reach the stage when I will say, 'This is what I believe. Finished.' What I believe is alive … and open to growth."

The Many Mystical Pathways. God joins the one and the many and speaks through all things. God is alive and constantly changing. Faithful through every season of life, God's mercies are new every morning. God can be approached in many ways. Moreover, God approaches us in many ways, changing God's approach as we change and initiating new possibilities to provoke changes in ourselves and the world. A personal God addresses each moment of creation intimately and uniquely, providing visions that are, as Alfred North Whitehead avers, the best possibility for each and every moment of experience, given its history, context, and previous decisions.

The varieties of religious experience and the plurality of spiritual traditions reflect God's creative-responsive love addressing cultures and spiritual leaders. Not a fall from grace, religious pluralism reflects the wonders of God's love and the infinity of divine creativity. Christ may be the way, the truth, and the life, but Christ's way is multi-faceted and excludes no authentic spiritual journey, as process theologian John Cobb asserts. Even when we turn from God, focusing on the devices and desires of our hearts, God still calls within our waywardness, inviting us to move from isolated individualism and self-interest to compassionate love and world loyalty.

Process theologian Jay McDaniel has articulated eight mystical paths. In the following paragraphs, I will explore, elaborate, and expand upon McDaniel's perceptive vision of the varieties of process-relational mystical experience.[19]

1. Mysticism of Inter-Connectedness. The whole universe conspires to create each moment of experience. We arise from the universe, from the Big Bang to the most recent encounter, and shape the universe by our own agency. We are part of a vast web of interconnectedness. As Jay McDaniel notes, deep down we sense that "each star, each planet, each blade of grass, each person — is a place where the whole of the universe is gathered into unity."

---

19 Mysticism: Eight Forms - Open Horizons, https://www.openhorizons.org/mysticism-eight-forms.html (last accessed November 12, 2023).

Process theology affirms that each moment and each creature is connected, indeed, present in and dependent upon everything else. Martin Luther King believed that ethics was grounded in the intricate interdependence of life.

> It all boils down to this, that all life is interrelated. We are caught in an inescapable network of mutuality, tied into a single garment of destiny. Whatever affects one directly, affects all indirectly. We are made to live together because of the interrelated structure of reality.[20]

The interconnectedness of life invites us to experience our lives a part of one vast and dynamic web in which every action radiates across the universe, shaping us and those around us. King continues, "For some strange reason I cannot be what I ought to be until you are what you ought to be. And you can never be what you ought to be until I am what I ought to be."[21] In the mysticism of interconnectedness, we feel empathy for every created life. There is no "other." Life is holy and the holiness of life evokes a sense of reverence for all creation. While Whitehead notes that creatures are often at cross purposes as prey and predator, we must minimize the pain other creatures experience. In the spirit of the Buddhist Bodhisattva, who chooses to be reborn until all creation is enlightened and all suffering ceases, the mysticism of relatedness expands our spirits to experience the joys and sorrows of all creation. The ebb and flow of the universe flows in and through us, and in our sense of unity with all creation, we choose to add to the beauty of life by acts of solidarity and lovingkindness.

2. *Mysticism of Local Community.* Related to the mysticism of interdependence, we affirm that love takes many forms — from the immediate circle of family to the larger circles of the non-human world, nation, and planet. Mysticism is always concretely rooted in a particular place, experiencing infinity in a grain of sand and in the face of your life companion. The Celtic saint Pelagius asserted that we could see the face of God in every newborn child. Bone of our bone and flesh of our flesh, we will sacrifice

---

20 Martin Luther King, *Testament of Hope* (New York: Harper One), 254.
21 *A Knock at Midnight* (New York: Warner Books, 2000), 208.

convenience, reputation, and life itself to save our children and grandchildren. We can also experience the holy in particular "thin places," as the Celts note, where a plot of land or stone formation becomes transparent to the Divine. Awakening from the dream of a ladder of angels, Jacob calls his place of revelation, Beth-El, the home or gateway to God.

While affirmation of the holiness of place and community can degenerate into idolatry, exclusion, and jingoistic nationalism, all mystical experiences join the local and the global. We encounter God in concrete situations as concrete persons and not as an abstraction revealed to persons in general. You can see the face of God in your beloved and find meaning in sacrificing for a greater good than oneself, in the welfare of a child, community, or nation. The mysticism of place and community is penultimate in nature, but its locality can inspire us to embrace God's presence everywhere and in all things. Love of family can lead to love of nation and planet. Our objects of love can become icons, windows into the Infinite, joining us with larger circles of relatedness. Our care for our grandchildren awakens responsibility to ensure a healthy environment for future generations of children we will never meet.

3. *Mysticism of Creative Energy.* The universe is energetic in nature. At times, we can feel a sense of bonding with the creative power, throbbing with life, of which all events and actualities are particularized manifestations. Whitehead calls the lively dynamic movement of life, Creativity, the constant advance into novelty, formless and yet aiming toward form. The mysticism of creative energy joins a sense that all things emerge out of energies of life and return to the creative process when their subjective immediacy passes away. It is the ever-flowing river of life, the womb of all creation, described as the Tao. The mysticism of creative energy invites us to immerse ourselves in the movement of life, in whom we live and move and have our being. We rejoice in the process of change itself, and our connectedness with the ever-flowing energy of life. Going with the flow of life, we also shape the flow of life by our commitment to bring beauty to the universe.

4. *Mysticism of Divine Archetypes.* This is the mysticism of possibility, the sense that there is, as McDaniel claims, "a realm of

timeless potentials — which are seen in the patterns which unfold in the universe, but which also transcend those patterns." While abstract in many ways, the realm of pure potentials is intuited in terms of Plato's Eternal Forms and Whitehead's Primordial Nature of God, the Divine Mind, which provides form and structure to the ongoing universe. Embracing the mind of God, our imaginations soar. We experience the confluence of order and stability and the equally dynamic and innovative movement of life whose contours reflect the marriage of eternal and unchanging possibility and ever-changing creativity. In apprehending directly divine possibility, all things take on an eternal aspect, and time becomes, as Plato affirms, "the moving image of eternity," and space becomes the "womb of possibility."

5. *Mysticism of Divine Love.* God is love and God's love births and evolves the universe. God has a personal relationship with every creature, and we can have an intimate and personal relationship with God. We can feel the heartbeat of God beating within our hearts, and we can, "walk with God and talk with God, and tell God we are God's own and the joy we share as we tarry there, none other has ever known."[22]

God's love is creative and responsive. Universal and intimate, God's love providentially guides our steps. Divine love also feels our joys and sorrows. God is our most intimate companion, and we rejoice in knowing "what a privilege it is to carry everything to God in prayer."[23]

Psalm 148 as well as Francis of Assisi's "Canticle of the Creatures" describe a world of praise in which all creatures give glory to their Intimate and Loving Creator.

> Praise the LORD!
> Praise the LORD from the heavens;
>   praise him in the heights!
> Praise God, all angels;
>   praise God, all God's host!
>   Praise God, sun and moon;
>   praise God, all you shining stars!

---

22 C. Austin Miles, "In the Garden."
23 Joseph M. Scriven, "What a Friend We Have in Jesus,"

Praise God, you highest heavens
and you waters above the heavens!...
Praise the LORD from the earth,
you sea monsters and all deeps,
fire and hail, snow and frost,
stormy wind fulfilling God's command!
Mountains and all hills,
fruit trees and all cedars!
Wild animals and all cattle,
creeping things and flying birds!
Kings of the earth and all peoples,
princes and all rulers of the earth!
Young men and women alike,
old and young together!

Francis of Assisi's hymn of praise echoes the Psalmist. Not only do all creatures praise God, but even death praises God as a portal to everlasting life.

Be praised, my Lord, through all your creatures,
especially through my lord Brother Sun,
who brings the day; and you give light through him...
Praise be You, my Lord, through Sister Moon
and the stars, in heaven you formed them
clear and precious and beautiful.
Praised be You, my Lord, through Brother Wind,
and through the air, cloudy and serene,
and every kind of weather through which
You give sustenance to Your creatures.
Praised be You, my Lord, through Sister Water,
whichis very useful and humble and precious and chaste.
Praised be You, my Lord, through Brother Fire,
through whom you light the night and he is beautiful
and playful and robust and strong.
Praised be You, my Lord, through Sister Mother Earth,
who sustains us and governs us and who produces
varied fruits with colored flowers and herbs...
Praised be You, my Lord,
through our Sister Bodily Death,
from whom no living man can escape.

Pentecostal worshippers chanting praise songs with raised hands and devotees of Krishna, chanting "Hare Krishna, Hare Rama," equally join their hearts with the loving heart of God. Buddhist devotees chanting to Amida Buddha as the source of salvation share in this same world of praise. The individual worshipper remains but their spirit expands to join the loving spirit of the creator and savior, who saves us when we cannot save ourselves.

6. *Mysticism of the Collective Unconscious.* We can intuit the whole universe in a grain of sand. We can also experience the whole history of the universe summed up in each moment of experience. Consciousness is the tip of the iceberg, undergirded by the vast, and almost infinite, unconscious realm which emerges in archetypes and dreams. Dreams are divine messages. Intuitions reveal the universe of experience flowing into our finite experiences. Angels and spirits guide our footsteps if we are attentive. As psychiatrist Carl Jung asserts, dreams and synchronous encounters guide our days and inspire us to personal and relational wholeness.

7. *Mysticism of Shamanic Journeying.* The human adventure is a vision quest in a world populated by spirits, talking animals, and the impact of good ancestors. The spirit world includes angels and demons and these creatures dwell within us and the non-human world. The shaman experiences the transcendent within daily life. The shaman soars to the heavens and dives to the underworld to receive spiritual messages and bring healing to the earth. The shaman has the gift of experiencing the unseen world of spiritual energy within the visible and palpable world of daily personal and communal life. The wisdom of paranormal experiences, whether from above or below, transforms personal and communal life. Within the realm of consciousness and the unconscious are many mansions, and there is a continuum of spiritual entities beyond human experience.

8. *Mysticism of Ordinary Life.* Brother Lawrence describes the mysticism of the "practice of the presence of God." In similar fashion, an earlier mystic Pierre de Caussade speaks of the "sacrament of the present moment." You can find yourself on holy ground doing homework with your grandchild as I do daily, washing the dishes and changing diapers, logging onto the internet, and paying

25

bills. The secular world of domestic tasks is holy, indeed, as Brother Lawrence notes, as holy as participating in the eucharist or holy communion. Every action can be done for the greater glory of God. Each encounter can be a way of doing something beautiful for God. If God is both omnipresent and omni-active, as process theology asserts, then every moment reveals God's presence for those whose senses are awakened. Enlightenment can occur in a monastery; it can also occur carpooling to work or picking a child up from school.

9. *Psychedelic Mysticism.* Spiritual adventures come in many forms. We can intuit the meaning of dreams, feel the deep peace of contemplative prayer and meditation, experience the transforming presence of God's love, and invest holiness in everyday tasks. God comes to us through both contemplation and also chemicals. For thousands of years, spiritual adventurers have drawn near to the Holy through the use of plant-based hallucinogens. These hallucinogens purify and open the doors of perception so that persons can experience divine messages and explore the many dimensions of life. Transcendental experiences, "your mind on plants," as Michael Pollan notes, place our lives in a cosmic context. The barriers confining the individual soul in the prison of mortality give way to the infinity of immortality. No longer afraid of death, we can live fully and courageously in the present moment.

Today, hospice residents as well as spiritual seekers use hallucinogens such as psilocybin to promote self-transcendence and greater peace of mind. A colleague of mine, after ingesting a small quantity of psylocibin (synthesized mushrooms) while attending a spiritual retreat, experienced his birth, and then felt that his individual conception was joined with the birth of the universe. He discovered that Spirit is eternal and that we are part of the vastness of universal energy and divine providence flowing through us. In life and death, we have nothing to fear.

In the late sixties, I ventured forth on the magical mystery tour, inspired by partaking of LSD, mescaline (synthesized peyote), and psilocybin (synthesized mushrooms). Though many of my "trips" were pleasurable and provided little spiritual insight, others involved soaring the heavens and descending to the underworld in ways similar to shamanic experience. My mind was "blown" and "expanded," and I felt a unity with all creation that still shapes my understanding of the universe. The wisdom and stature I experienced through hallucinogens in the 1960's opened me to the transpersonal world and activated my imagination. Divine possibilities emerged over the past five decades that would not have occurred apart from my youthful use of psychedelics.

10. *A Spirituality of the Senses.* Embodied experience is at the heart of process theology as well as mysticism. God's grandeur reveals itself in every experience, mind, body, and spirit. The senses are portals to divinity, reflective of God's presence in all things. Despite the realities of change and mortality, the body is as real as spirit. The spirit is embodied, and the body is inspired. God is incarnate in all things. The Word became flesh and dwells in our world. We are words of God, whose cells and souls alike reveal God's presence. We can experience embodied divinity through practicing Tai Chi, Qi Gong, Reiki healing touch, and Hatha Yoga.

LIVING PROCESS MYSTICISM

It has been said that most people are ecstasy deficient. They don't experience the wonder of the universe and their own individual existence. They pass the color purple, a sunset, or a tree flaming with autumn color and without noticing their beauty. Power and possession seem more important than beauty. In contrast, process mysticism affirms the insight of Fyodor Dostoevsky, who asserted that "the world is saved by beauty." In that spirit, process theologian and spiritual guide Patricia Adams Farmer invites us to take regular "beauty breaks," perhaps daily or throughout the day, when we simply pause, notice, open to, and embrace the beauty in and around us. Such experiences fill the senses and mediate God to us. The whole earth is filled with God's glory, and in awakening to beauty, we are amazed at life and choose reverence and gratitude rather than manipulation and control.

In this practice, simply pause throughout the day to take a few moments to "Behold" the beauty of the world. You may discover author Annie Dillard's "tree with lights" or spend a few minutes with poet Mary Oliver transfixed by a grasshopper in a meadow.

You may notice with Gerard Manley the "pied beauty" of dappled things and discover that the world is charged with "God's grandeur." Awaken to wonder, beauty, amazement, and the creative love of the Divine Artist moving through your life and all creation.

CHAPTER FOUR

INTO THE MYSTIC

Philosophy is mystical. For mysticism is depths as yet un-spoken. But the purpose of philosophy is to rationalize mysticism; not by explaining it away, but by the introduction of novel verbal characterizations, rationally coordinated.[24]

Process mysticism embraces body, mind, spirit, and relation-ships, and love of the good earth. Grounded in solitude, it inspires commitment to the well-being of the planet and social responsi-bility. Mysticism transcends any religious tradition and practice. Mystical experiences may come unexpectedly and dramatically. Moses encounters a burning bush, from which the Holy One speaks. Isaiah is astounded by Divine Revelation in the Jerusalem Temple. Paul falls off his horse when he experiences the Light of Christ. Mary of Magdala is astounded and comes alive when she hears Jesus calling her name in the Garden.

Mysticism may also emerge through a commitment to reg-ular spiritual practices. Gradually and undramatically, the doors of perception are cleansed, and we experience the beauty and in-finity of the universe and ourselves. The veil is lifted through our intentionality and the Word becomes flesh in our daily lives. All things become charged with God's grandeur through a lifetime of prayerful contemplation. Suffering and attachment are extin-guished, and we experience the freedom of the Holy Moment, as Buddha did after weeks of meditation under the Bodhi Tree.

Whether their encounters with God are bidden or unbidden, gradual or dramatic, most seekers nurture ongoing experiences of the Holy through contemplative practices. Process mysticism in-spires a variety of spiritual practices, all of which open us to the ubiquity of Divine Revelation and join our experiences of the God of images with the God beyond our imagination. Dazzling dark-ness meets brilliant light in our encounter with the Living and Multi-Faceted God. In this section, I will explore a few spiritu-

---

24 Alfred North Whitehead, *Modes of Thought* (New York: Free Press, 1968), 174.

al practices, congruent with my experience of process mysticism. My list is far from exhaustive. In fact, these practices came to me intuitively on my contemplative predawn walks as a response to my prayer for intellectual guidance in writing this book. Other process theologians would lift up different practices. Implicit in my list is the importance of silent, breath, and centering prayers as ways of experiencing the Holy. Just as God personally addresses us, we can discover spiritual practices appropriate to our time, place, faith tradition, age, and season of life.

Reiki Healing Touch and the Mysticism of Healing Energy. Process theology proclaims a living, feeling, empathetic universe. The universality of experience points to the lively and experiential interdependence of mind, body, and spirit. Spirit is embodied and the body is inspired. Physical touch can transform our bodies as well as our minds. Reiki healing touch, along with practices such as Tai Chi, Qi Gong, and Therapeutic/healing Touch, are forms of prayer and mysticism in movement. As a Reiki practitioner and teacher since the 1980s, my daily practice of self-reiki awakens me to the subtle and interdependent energies of life following through me and the universe. When I give a hands-on or distant Reiki treatment to someone, I am awakening my own and another's experience of the Energy of Love (chi, ki, prana, ruach, breath of life) that flows in and through all things. Prayerful touch opens us to the holiness of embodiment and cleanses the doors of perception, opening us to the mystic energies of incarnation and interdependence.[25]

Kything, or Deep Empathy. Grounded in a Scottish word coined by Madeleine L'Engle is "a spiritual act of conscious presence" with another across time and space.[26] The graceful interdependence of life joins every creature. Non-local in nature and grounded in process theology's vision of causation at an unconscious level, joining

---

25 For more on Reiki healing touch, see Bruce Epperly *The Energy of Love: Reiki and Christian Healing* (Gonzales: FL: Energion, 2017) and *Reiki Healing Touch and the Way of Jesus* (Kelowna, BC: Northstone Books, 2005, with Kate Epperly).

26 Louis Savary and Patrician Berne, *Kything: The Art of Spiritual Presence* (Mahwah, NJ: Paulist Press, 1988), 7.

us despite physical distance, kything is "spirit-to-spirit" presence.[27] In kything, we experience our empathetic communication with all creation as it is focused on a particular relationship. This form of empathetic understanding, or spiritual unity, involves a flexible three-step process: 1) centering, 2) focusing imaginatively or empathetically on another, and 3) establishing a spiritual connection or union through awareness of companionship across space and time. When I kythe, a practice similar to intercessory prayer, I visualize the other beside me, spiritually joined, and sharing love with one another. We are one in the Spirit and at a deep unconscious level, we are connected even beyond the grave.

Seeing the World. The mysticism of the senses simply involves delighting in the world. If the aim of God, is toward the production of beauty, then creation in its many forms reveals beauty. When I take a "beauty break," as theologian and pastor Patricia Adams Farmer counsels, I simply let my senses delight in the wonder of creation — sight, smell, taste, touch, sound.

With Beauty All Around Me I Walk. A Navajo (diné) Prayer of Blessing proclaims that God is found in movement. When our bodies move, our spirits also move. New horizons emerge, thoughts and feelings shift, changes happen, when I walk open to the divine in all things.

> With beauty before me I walk
> With beauty behind me I walk
> With beauty above me I walk
> With beauty around me I walk…

Solvitur Ambulando, as Augustine of Hippo asserted. "It will be solved in the walking," and in the walking, we discover that our feet are always on holy ground. In walking prayers, we may join our breath, inhaling and exhaling with each step. We may also simply spend our walk giving thanks, praying for others, or delighting the senses and the world around us. *Centering.* Process theology affirms that God is the Alpha and Omega of each moment of experience. Although freedom and creativity are present at every level of experience, and most especially

27 Ibid., 17.

at the commitment to spiritual transformation, each moment of experience emerges from God's vision of what it can become, given its environment and previous decisions. God's presence is intimate and personal, seeking the "best for that impasse," the highest possibility for this moment and the future in every situation.

In moments of centering, we pause in order to pay attention to God's presence in our lives. The key word for centering is to be still and pay attention to the Holiness of the Moment, incarnate in your life and the world around you. This can be done through following the Psalmist's counsel, "be still and know that I am God." It may also emerge through various forms of centering prayer, involving the repetition of words, scriptures, mantras, or focus on images to pierce "the cloud of unknowing," so that we can experience the Holiness and Vision of each particular moment. God's spiritual and moral arcs flow through all things, revealing God's vision for history, our communities, and our personal lives. In centering contemplation, we glimpse the divine arc within and around us and are given the opportunity to allow God's arc to define our experiences and actions.

Lovingkindness. The apostle Paul proclaims that we are all part of the dynamically interdependent "body of Christ." Buddhist teachers, such as Thich Nhat Hanh, speak of interbeing, the living web of life from which each moment arises to which each moment contributes. In lovingkindness, we affirm our connection with the world around us in all its tragic beauty. Our neighbor's joys delight us. Our neighbor's pain saddens us. The boundary between self and other is real, but permeable. *Ubuntu,* "I am because of you. You are because of me. We are because of one another." Thomas Merton reveals the spirit of lovingkindness in a mystical experience that awakened him to the love that moves the stars and galaxies, and gives birth to every heartbeat.

> ...at the corner of Fourth and Walnut, in the center of the shopping district, I was suddenly overwhelmed with the realization that I loved all those people, that they were mine and I was theirs, that we could not be alien to one another even though we were total strangers.
> It was like waking from a dream of separateness... The

whole illusion of separate holy existence is a dream.[28]

Our love for one another reflects God's love for us and inspires certain mystics to discover God through devotional mysticism. The Hare Krishna monk chants "Hare Krishna, Hare Rama," to join their heart with the Heart of the Universe. The evangelical Christian, inspired by God's love embodied in Jesus of Nazareth and the quest for a personal relationship with Jesus, aligns their soul with "love divine, all love excelling,"[29] and bursts forth in song, "This is my story, this is my song, praising my savior all the day long."[30] "God is love" (1 John 4:8) and the fellow sufferer who understands and intimate companion who rejoices may be found in joining with all creation in a world of praise, affirming with the Psalmist, "let everything that breathes, praise God" (Psalm 150:6).

Going with the Flow. The process is the reality. Movement is the heart of life. All things flow. While order, tradition, intention, and practice, are essential to the mystic's journey, so is aimlessness and dependence solely on the Graceful Interdependence of Life. "Amazing grace, how sweet the sound,"[31] inspires the mysticism of flow. "Leaning on the everlasting arms,"[32] we experience friendship with all creation. God's flow in its tragic beauty, the movements of the Tao in their emergent dynamism, give life to all things. In letting the river of life flow in and through us, we experience without effort wonder, beauty, interdependence, and the movements of the divine arc of justice. Creativity, the many becoming one in each moment of life, pushes us forward, and trusting the process awakens us to the wonder of each breath. All shall be well. After a week of intentionality running a business, guiding the government, or teaching a class in the spirit of the orderly Confucius, we let go and let flow with the Taoist sages at day's end and on the weekend. We discover that we must be children, living in the Holy Here and Holy Now, to experience the fullness of God's realm. Letting the child within out to play, and inspiring other children to have the resources to play awakens us to the playful nature of Spirit. God

28 Thomas Merton, *Essential Writings* (Maryknoll, NY: Orbis Books, 2000), *90.*
29 Charles Wesley, "Love Divine."
30 Fanny J. Crosby, "Blessed Assurance."
31 John Newton, "Amazing Grace.
32 Elisha Hoffman, "Leaning on the Everlasting Arms."

creates the galaxies and guides the moral arc, God also whimsically participates in the evolutionary process, bringing forth storks and ostriches, pangolins and panda bears, leaping whales and children at play. In playful trust, we experience the joyfulness of God moving within the varieties of galaxies, creatures, cultures, music, and spirituality. With the Flying Scot, Eric Liddell, celebrated in the film "Chariots of Fire," we can exclaim "God made me fast [or a writer, singer, athlete, knitter, and so forth] and when I run, I feel God's pleasure." God with skin, fully creaturely and fully divine, rejoices in the color purple, loving embraces, meandering about on a summer day rejoicing in a grasshopper,[33] and the mere fact of breathing. "Not all those who wander are lost," as J.R.R. Tolkien avers, and as we flow with divine energy, we discover the Deep Mystery flowing in and through us.

Mysticism and Psychedelics. The use of psychedelics and hallucinogens for spiritual transformation has been part of humankind's spiritual journey for thousands of years. Shamanic leaders and First Americans ingested peyote and various other hallucinogens as part of religious ritual, enabling the participant more fully to experience sacred wisdom, journey from the heavens to the underworld, and solve problems in this lifetime. In the United States, the Native American Church joins the use of peyote and native spirituality with Christian faith, grounded in the belief that the Great Spirit created peyote for medicinal, healing, and spiritual purposes. Taken in a manner similar to the Christian sacraments, within the rituals a faith community and as a spiritual practice, peyote enlivens and enlightens the practitioner's vision of reality and ability to respond to the challenges of life. Today, the use of psychedelics, including derivatives of peyote and mushrooms, mescaline and psilocybin, is being studied in hospice settings to enable persons to experience self-transcendence which decreases death anxiety. A growing number of Christians have integrated the use of psychedelics as sacramental vehicles of spiritual transcendence.[34]

---

33 Mary Oliver, "The Summer Day."
34 For example, Ligare: A Christian Psychedelic Society — https://www. ligare.org/ (last accessed November 12, 2023.

In describing his own experiences with mescaline, *The Doors of Perception,* Aldous Huxley quotes the wisdom of William Blake, "if the doors of perception were cleansed everything would appear to man as it is: Infinite." The mind, according to Huxley, is a reducing valve, necessary for survival. The radical amazement of sheer becoming – the wonder of our being and the reality of all things – needs to be channeled to operate motor vehicles, cook breakfast, get our children ready for school, and go to work. Yet, as process theology affirms, daily consciousness is the tip of the iceberg, undergirded by the vastness of the universe flowing into our unconscious and the ever-present wisdom of God seeking to guide our steps. Mystical moments, whether spontaneous, induced by the spiritually guided use of psychedelics, or the result of years of contemplation and spiritual reflection, emerge when our spirits are opened to the wider vistas of reality, the Energy of Love which created the universe, the Divine Providence which constantly supplies wisdom, and the amazing reality of every created thing.

While I strongly believe that the use of psychedelics must be controlled and requires the presence of an experienced spiritual companion and quality control of the hallucinogens ingested, psychedelics can awaken us to "the Spirit's sighs too deep for words." The sacramental use of psychedelics, like contemplative spiritual practices, open us to the deeper transpersonal realities, beneath and beyond the conscious mind. They may help us glimpse the "mind of God," opening us to a Wisdom Deeper than Our Own.

Process theology welcomes the mystic in each of us and supports spiritual practices that enable us to live holistically and lovingly. Mystical experiences are not exceptional or supernatural but reflect God's constant movements – the divine possibilities and compassionate communities – in our lives and the world.

LIVING PROCESS THEOLOGY

God comes to us in many ways. Virtually every appreciative and positive action can be a doorway to Divinity. People experience God in giving a child a bath, running on a beach, and, with Brother Lawrence, working in the monastery kitchen and discovering common chores can be eucharistic in nature. In the previous sections, I have presented a number of contemplative practices involving healing touch, opening the senses to beauty, empathy, compassionate care, and sacramental use of hallucinogens. You may choose to do something countercultural, like going with the flow or experiencing your unity with another person through kything or learning Reiki healing touch. Explore various mystical methods in the weeks ahead.

CHAPTER FIVE

HEAVENLY MINDED AND EARTHLY GOOD

Religion is world loyalty... God is that function in the world by reason of which our purposes are directed to ends which in our own consciousness are impartial to our own interests... of which our purposes extend beyond values to ourselves to values to others.[35]

Process mysticism is holistic. It defies legalisms, dualisms, and stereotypes. Mystics retreat from the world to a life of prayer, but their praying in the context of an interdependent universe transforms the spiritual temperature of the planet, tipping the balance from violence to peace and death to life. Religion is, as Whitehead asserts, what a person does with their solitariness. Solitariness is not isolation. The mystic's withdrawal gives rise to widening circles of empathy and self-transcending selfhood. Mysticism inspires the movement from transactional and individual salvation and personal prosperity to world loyalty. Paul's meditation on the energetic body of Christ, the church community and the world as church, asserts "If one member suffers, all suffer together with it; if one member is honored, all rejoice together with it." (1 Corinthians 12:26)

The great mystics of the contemporary world – Dorothy Day, Oscar Romero, Peace Pilgrim, Dag Hammarskjold, Thich Nhat Hanh, Mahatma Gandhi, Martin Luther King, Abraham Joshua Heschel, Dietrich Bonhoeffer, and Mother (Saint) Teresa – joined prayer and protest and contemplation and action to set at liberty the oppressed, free the captives, and proclaim the day of God's Shalom and Liberation.[36]

Solitude and social concern, the journey inward and journey outward, are the yin and yang of contemplative activism. Aligned with the spirit of Alfred North Whitehead, one of my spiritual mentors Howard Thurman notes "All life is one, and yet life moves

---

35 Alfred North Whitehead, *Religion in the Making*, 59, 151-152.
36 For more on contemplative activism, see Bruce Epperly, *Mystics in Action: Twelve Saints for Today* (Maryknoll, NY: Orbis, 2021).

in such intimate circles of awful individuality. The power of life perhaps is its aloneness.... Each soul must learn to stand up in its own right and live.... We walk a part of the way together, but on the upper reaches of life, each path takes its way to the heights – alone."[37]

Process theology counsels what Thurman's teacher Rufus Jones described as "affirmative mysticism," prophetic spirituality that seeks to embody God's realm "on earth as it is in heaven." In the spirit of process mysticism, Thurman, whose *Jesus and the Disinherited* may have been the first black liberation theology, claims that "mysticism is the response of the individual to a personal encounter with God within his own soul...such response is total, effecting the inner quality of life and its outward expression."[38] Recognizing that mysticism inspires greater empathy, the mystic challenges anything that prevents people from experiencing abundant life. Thurman continues, "social action, therefore is an expression of resistance against whatever tends to, or separates one, from the experience of God, who is the ground of the [mystic's] being." The mystic's social agenda is grounded in the intricate interdependence of life, most especially revealed in the impact of social institutions and business practices, on persons' wellbeing. The mystic seeks "the removal of all that prevents God from coming to himself in the individual. Whatever there is that blocks this, calls for action."[39]

Aware that God is present in all creation, and that God is working for the "best for that impasse" in oppressor and oppressed alike, the mystic seeks the redemption and wholeness of all persons. Beyond incivility and polarization, the mystic's protest of injustice or planetary destruction is aimed at the prophetic healing of all of God's beloved, even those who perpetrate injustice. Injustice and oppression destroy the souls of both the oppressor and oppressed and limit the effectiveness of God's vision in their lives.

---

37 Howard Thurman, *Deep is the Hunger* (Richmond IN: Friends United, 1978), 169.

38 Howard Thurman, *Mysticism and Social Action: Lawrence Lectures and Discussions with Howard Thurman* (London: IARF, 2014), Kindle Location, 177-179.

39 Ibid., Kindle Location, 235-236, 244-245.

Jesus is illuminated on the Mount of Transfiguration and descends to the flatlands only to be confronted by a panic-stricken father whose child needs healing. Moses encounters God in a burning bush and is called to liberate his people. Martin Luther King hears God's voice of assurance in his most desperate hour and commits to leading the Montgomery Boycott, knowing that God will be with him regardless of the outcome. On the eve of his death, as if inspired by a paranormal experience, King speaks of the value of longevity and also rejoices that he has seen God's promised land and that even if he does not make it to the promised land, God's truth will march onward.

The world depends on mystics, whose peace comes, as Whitehead notes, from joining the individual self and its concerns with concerns greater than one's own, the wellbeing of the planet and its creatures and alignment with God's peace that marches forward guided by the vision of truth, goodness, and beauty.

LIVING PROCESS MYSTICISM

Mysticism inspires world loyalty. Mystics experience greater empathy and unity with the world around them. Often we don't know how to join compassion with social concern. In this practice, begin by asking God to guide you to a particular need in your community, nation, or the world. Ask for a vision and guidance in terms of how to use your compassion to change the world as God's companion in healing the earth. There are many needs and many paths. Although I am not a prophet or activist by inclination, my prayers for guidance have led me to use my skill as a writer to reflect on biblical resources for social transformation, most recently in my *The Prophet Amos Speaks to America,* and in a future book in this series *Process Theology and Prophetic Faith.* I have also begun to teach classes on social issues to laypersons and am using my academic skills to promote responses to climate change.

Pray for guidance and then let the events of your life become icons opening you to divine inspiration and practical responses to the world's suffering.

BOOKS FOR THE MYSTIC JOURNEY

John Buchanan, *Processing Reality: Finding Meaning in Death, Psychedelics, and Sobriety* (Eugene Oregon: Cascade Books, 2022).

Daniel Dombrowski, *Process Mysticism* (Albany: SUNY Press, 2023).

Bruce Epperly, *Mystics in Action: Twelve Saints for Today* (Orbis Press, 2021)

Bruce Epperly, *Process Theology: Embracing Adventure with God* (Gonzalez, FL: Energion, 2014).

Bruce Epperly, *Process Theology: A Guide for the Perplexed* (London: T &T Clark, 2011).

Bruce Epperly, *Process Spirituality: Practicing Holy Adventure* (Gonzalez, FL: Energion, 2017).

Bruce Epperly, *The Mystic in You: Discovering a God-filled World* (Nashville: Upper Room, 2018).

Patricia Adams Farmer, *Embracing a Beautiful God: Tenth Anniversary Edition* (Create Space, 2013).

David Ray Griffin, *Parapsychology, Philosophy, and Spirituality: A Postmodern Exploration* (Albany: SUNY Press, 1997).

Catherine Keller, *The Cloud of the Impossible: Negative Theology and Planetary Entanglement* (New York: Columbia University Press, 2014).

Jay McDaniel, *Living from the Center: Spirituality in an Age of Consumerism* (St. Louis: Chalice Press, 2000).

Marjorie Suchocki, *In God's Presence: Theological Reflections on Prayer* (St. Louis: Chalice Press, 1996).

www.ingramcontent.com/pod-product-compliance
Lightning Source LLC
Chambersburg PA
CBHW011747020426
42331CB00014B/3312